GO

You're New Again

So

You're New Again

How to Succeed When You Change Jobs

Elwood F. Holton III

Sharon S. Naquin

BK

BERRETT-KOEHLER PUBLISHERS, INC.
San Francisco

Berrett-Koehler Publishers, Inc.
450 Sansome Street, Suite 1200
San Francisco, CA 94111-3320
Tel: (415) 288-0260   Fax: (415) 362-2515   www.bkconnection.com

ORDERING INFORMATION

Quantity Sales. Special discounts are available on quantity purchases by corporations, associations, and others. For details, contact the "Special Sales Department" at the Berrett-Koehler address above.

Individual Sales. Berrett-Koehler publications are available through most bookstores. They can also be ordered direct from Berrett-Koehler: Tel: (800) 929-2929; Fax: (802) 864-7626; www.bkconnection.com.

Orders for college textbook/course adoption use. Please contact Berrett-Koehler: Tel: (800) 929-2929; Fax: (802) 864-7626.

Orders by U.S. trade bookstores and wholesalers. Please contact Publishers Group West, 1700 Fourth Street, Berkeley, CA 94710. Tel: (510) 528-1444; Fax: (510) 528-3444.

Printed in the United States of America

Printed on acid-free and recycled paper that is composed of 85% recovered fiber, including 15% postconsumer waste.

Library of Congress Cataloging-in-Publication Data

Holton, Elwood F., 1957–
  So you're new again: how to succeed when you change jobs /
Elwood F. Holton III, Sharon S. Naquin.
    p. cm.
  ISBN 1-58376-169-1
  1. Vocational guidance. 2. Career development. 3. Work—Psychological aspects.
I. Naquin, Sharon S. II. Title.
  HF5381 .H576 2000
  650.14—dc21
                              00-011217

First Edition

05 04 03 02 01 00   10 9 8 7 6 5 4 3 2 1

Cover and Interior Design: Bookwrights Design
Editorial Services: PeopleSpeak
Indexing: Directions Unlimited

To our families:
Karen, Karie, and Melanie Holton
and
Al and Blair Naquin

Contents

Preface

Careers are full of transitions—to new departments, to new organizations, to different types of jobs, from staff positions to management. Each one puts you in the position of being a "new employee" again. Most people think of a new employee as one who changes to a new company, but in reality the label applies anytime you move to a new role, whether within an organization or between organizations. This book is written for all experienced employees who find themselves in the position of being new again.

Ironically, the more experienced we are, the less we think about how to be an effective new employee and the less we remember about how to do it well. Experience seduces us into thinking that we don't have to worry about being new. The truth is that *every* employee, from a staff person to a CEO, has to work on the new employee transition. One only has to look at very visible failures at the CEO level to realize that problems with employee transition do not discriminate by job level, pay, or amount of experience.

This book arose out of our seeing the frustrations and mistakes made by many experienced new employees. We know that a little bit of learning can make an incredible difference and that those who learn how to be new again can avoid costly mistakes, obtain better opportunities, and become more successful. We know this from our experience, our interviews with new employees at all levels, and from research. The message from all sources is clear: what you do as a new employee really matters.

Over the past twelve years we have used the twelve-step process described in this book to coach countless employees on how to make a better start. The really good news is that, for most, learning a better way to start a new job was a personal relief and a boost to their careers. We know this system works. Our challenge in this book was to package our advice in a concise, user-friendly format so readers could quickly learn the system in today's hurry-up world. We hope that this book helps many experienced new employees get the best start possible in their new positions. Good luck!

Elwood F. Holton III
Sharon S. Naquin
Baton Rouge, Louisiana

One

So You're New Again

Congratulations! You have decided to make a career transition, either by changing jobs within your organization or moving to a new organization. As a result, you are about to be a new employee again. This can be an exciting yet scary time. This book is designed to help you learn how to make the most of this career change. There's no question that your success in your new position will be based in large part on your skills and abilities. But skills and abilities alone are not enough to make a successful transition. How well you manage being "new" again will play a much bigger role than you think in making your career change a success.

Consider this situation:

Paul, an employee just beginning his second month of work with a new company, was stunned. His boss, the vice president, had called him in to discuss her "concern with his progress and ability to operate as a team player." She informed him that his colleagues had complained that he was too cocky, too outspoken, and too critical of their work processes. Behind his back, his colleagues referred to him as the "we used to" guy. They claimed that Paul prefaced almost every comment regarding their current processes with "We used to do it a better way at my old company." He would continue with a lengthy description of his previous employer's methodologies and praise for the merits of the "old and better" way. Paul considered his comments to be suggestions for improvement. He thought he was being helpful and showing his ability. However, his colleagues interpreted his comments as overly critical, arrogant, and disparaging.

This type of situation occurs in all types of organizations. Most job changers work hard during the job search process and take their careers seriously. Many find good positions and start work with high levels of energy and enthusiasm. They are optimistic about the possibilities that their new jobs hold and try hard to make a good impression. Unfortunately, however, many are disappointed. Why? Because most of them overlook a critical step, which will make much of the hard work that went into finding a job worthless. Like Paul, they haven't learned how to make the transition from experienced employee to new employee.

Does that sound a little strange? All of your previous experience can only help you in your new job, right? Far from it, although most job changers assume just that. Most managers and executives we interviewed complain that new employees (both new graduates and employees with experience) don't understand what it takes to successfully enter and adapt to a new organization. Experienced employees are particularly prone to overlook the fact that they are starting over again when they change organizations. Whether you are just starting a new job, getting ready to make a change, or still in your first year on a new job, this book can help.

What Do You Know?

Before you go any further in this book, here's a little quiz to see where you stand. Begin by writing "true" or "false" beside each statement below. The correct answers are at the end of the next section—but no cheating!

1. The number one problem most employers have with their new hires is that they don't learn the tasks of their jobs quickly enough.

2. The best strategy to make a good impression on your new employer is to try to find something really outstanding to do.

3. It is important that you get past the new employee stage as quickly as you can.

4. The lessons you learned in your previous organization will be welcome suggestions for change in your new company.

5. You can count on your boss to help you get started.

6. Being a new employee is not as hard when you have previous work experience.

7. Your coworkers will be happy to have you join the group.

8. It's good to let people know quickly what your style of working is so they can adjust.

9. Your boss will have a pretty good idea of how you can be most productive.

10. Because of your experience, you should be quick to point out mistakes when you see them.

So You Don't Think You Are Really New

New employees with experience are often the first to think they are not *really* new. Yet many employees we interviewed commented on how little they remembered about starting a new job and how much they wish they had been reminded when they changed jobs. Why? Because when you change jobs, you really are new, even if you have lots of experience in another organization. Worse yet, sometimes the experience you have already gained actually makes entering a new organization harder and leads you to make more than the usual number of mistakes.

This paradox can be traced to the concept of organizational culture. Organizations are social systems that create cultures and subcultures. Organizational culture includes a set of assumptions that group members have learned and that worked well for them in the past. Furthermore, the group seeks to teach these assumptions to new members as the correct way to think and act. Thus, culture is a powerful force that must be understood. It manifests itself in many forms, including norms, beliefs, language, rites, stories, rituals, and symbols. To become a high performer, employees entering an organization must learn behaviors that fit the new culture and unlearn behaviors that fit previous employers' cultures.

Organizations also develop multiple subcultures around occupational groups, geographic locations, departments, informal groups, hierarchical status, expertise, and so on. Subcultures may arise within certain levels of an organization (staff, manager, etc.). Thus, line workers will have a different subculture than first-line supervisors, who in turn will have a different subculture than managers. Subcultures also may develop within or between separate departments, divisions, or other functional groups. Another type of subculture may arise within different social circles in an organization. For example, long-term, trusted employees will have unique cultural characteristics that new employees won't have.

Every time you cross a "boundary" between subcultures or cultures (e.g., entering a new organization or a new department) you are new and have to adapt. Subculture changes, such as transferring from one department to another, are usually easier because you are still part of the same larger culture. Changes from one organization to another may entail huge culture differences. Professional careers usually consist of a series of these boundary crossings as people move between departments, are promoted, become increasingly valued and trusted, or move from one company to another.

A new employee then is simply one who has crossed an organizational boundary and must perform in a new organizational culture or subculture. In this sense, a fifteen-year employee who advances to a new level of management is only slightly different from a new hire from outside the company. Both have crossed organizational boundaries into new cultures. While the scope and content of their adaptation may differ, the fundamental steps for the employees to develop to high performance do not. In some cases, internal boundary crossings may create more significant adaptation problems than an external boundary crossing. For example, a line worker who is promoted to first-line supervisor may face a more significant culture change entering his or her first managerial role than taking a similar line-worker position at another company.

Most likely, you are reading this book because you have changed organizations or changed jobs within your organization, and that is the way we will frame most of our discussion. However, remember that the skills and adaptation process discussed here are ones you will use throughout your career. The best employees become quite skilled at entering different groups and companies. You are new now and you will be new many times in your career. Interestingly, being a newcomer never gets any easier. Even some CEOs have failed because they did not adapt to a new culture quickly enough. We will discuss culture and how you learn it in more detail throughout this book.

At the end of the last section, you completed a short quiz. Did you answer all the questions with "false"? If so, you were correct. Don't feel bad if you didn't get them all right. Many people do not. That little quiz should remind you that some time spent relearning how to be new is time well spent.

The Unique First Year

As you probably remember from your previous experiences, starting to work in a new organization requires a special perspective and special strategies for success. First and foremost, new employees need to recognize and accept that the first year on a new job represents a separate and distinct career stage. It's a transition period that must be considered separately from the rest of the career ladder. This is true regardless of how many years of experience you may have. The only way to make sense of what happens during this time is by considering the first year on the job separately from the rest of the career ladder.

From the time that you accept your new job offer until about the end of the first six to twelve months, you will be in an intermediate transition stage. What happens at that stage can have a huge impact on your career. While it is all too easy to cling to old (and possibly unrealistic) expectations, wise new employees recognize the importance of letting them go. They realize that it takes time to earn the rights, responsibilities, and credibility of a full-fledged member of the organization, regardless of their previous work experience.

You will be closely scrutinized during this transition period. Because you are the newcomer (even with lots of experience), your colleagues will treat you differently from others: they will respond to you differently, work with you differently, and judge you differently. Everything you do or say will be watched with a critical eye. You must follow a different set of rules to succeed during this breaking-in stage. You can no longer rely on the old rules that helped you attain success in your previous job. That was Paul's problem in the earlier scenario: he didn't understand that only by learning the new rules could he get a strong start in his new job.

You undoubtedly want to start off on the right foot in your new organization. No one begins a job expecting to fail, but what can you do to help ensure that you stay out of trouble and project a professionally mature image right from the start? Learning the new "rules" is essential. Unfortunately, few new employees take the time to learn them, so they start their new jobs all wrong. If you are a wise new employee, you'll recognize this as a golden opportunity to distinguish yourself from other new hires and excel by showing your professional maturity.

Does It Really Matter?

We can't emphasize enough how much of an impact the first year has on your success within an organization. The impressions you make on your manager and colleagues in your first weeks and months will play a major role in your career opportunities and success within that organization. Research suggests that how you approach your first year will impact your performance, future salary, advancement, job satisfaction, and ability to move within the organization, as well as your own feelings of success and commitment to the job. It can affect your career for many years to come.

Your challenge in the early months will be to earn the respect of your colleagues and establish your reputation as a bright, capable, and valuable employee. If you are successful, you will quickly be given opportunities to make bigger contributions to the organization and to make yourself more visible to upper management. If you then take advantage of those early opportunities by demonstrating what an outstanding performer you are, more opportunities to succeed will follow. Edgar Schein, a noted management author, called this the "success spiral," and you want to get on it! The strategies discussed in this book will help you accomplish this goal.

Make too many mistakes and you may find your career derailed. That is, instead of being on the success spiral, you will be in a holding pattern while bosses and colleagues decide how much potential you really have. Unfortunately, the pressure on experienced hires is greater than on those with little or no experience. People tend to assume that your experience has taught you how to adjust to a new job quickly. In fact, the opposite may be true. How you enter an organization is so important that many executives privately suggest that the best strategy if you get off to a bad start is to find another job. That's not to say that an entire thirty-year career is made or broken in a few months' performance. However, the simple fact is that it can take years to recover from a poor start.

Two

What's Really Important in the First Year

f you are like most new employees, you're probably thinking a lot about the tasks you've been hired to do. Guess what your employer is worried about? Not your ability to do the *tasks* but rather your ability to do the *nontask* components of the job. These components include your willingness and ability to learn new ideas, fit into the organization's culture, earn respect and credibility, learn the politics of the organization, build effective working relationships, become an accepted member of the organization, learn the informal structure and methods of the company, discover what the unwritten expectations are, understand the power-and-reward structure, and learn how to accomplish work within the organization. Most employers (particularly large ones) are very good at hiring people whom they believe have the raw talent and ability to perform the basic tasks of their jobs. Plus, your experience and track record tell them that you have the ability to do the job.

When managers of new employees are asked what makes the difference between an *average* new employee and an *outstanding* new employee, task performance has little to do with the answers. Outstanding new employees, they say, are the ones who have the right attitudes, get along well with new coworkers, learn about the organization quickly, fit in, and exhibit other characteristics we will discuss here. The conclusion: most new employees are focused on the wrong elements of a job!

The twelve-step system outlined below will help you focus on the nontask elements of the job that should be high priorities for new employees. Many of these may be familiar to you, but they are easy to forget if it has been a while since you were last a new employee. Furthermore, the notion of new employee transition skills is unfamiliar to many people, so even lots of experience may not have prepared you to be great at being new.

Unlearning: The Key to Your Success

Nobody talks about unlearning your way to success, but new learning often can't occur until you unlearn old ways. In many aspects, unlearning is much harder than learning because you have to let go of the assumptions, behaviors, and attitudes that may have helped you be quite successful in the past.

You might be thinking, "Wait a minute, I was hired because of my experience and previous success. Shouldn't I use that experience?" This is where the problem occurs. If you're thinking about your ability to perform the functions of your job (e.g., engineering, computer programming, selling, financial analysis), then you are absolutely correct. You were hired because of your functional experience, and you should use it to help the new organization. But—here comes the paradox—when it comes to the organization's culture and ways of doing business, you must unlearn most of what you know about your old organization and learn the new culture!

Cultural knowledge does not transfer well, and you cannot learn it without first unlearning. For example, if your old organization was very informal and one "rule" was that you could visit with any manager at any level to discuss a problem, you have probably internalized that as the "right" way to solve problems. Suppose your new organization is more formal and the protocol is that you go through the proper channels before talking to your manager's boss. Until you unlearn the old protocol, you will probably apply the old norm to the new organization—and make a big mistake!

For this reason, the new employee process can be conceived of as having three stages: *initiation, transition,* and *adaptation.* The key tasks and issues of each stage are listed in table 1 below. Initiation is the period during which you realize the number of cultural norms you have internalized that won't work in your new organization. If you are like most people, you won't think you have internalized many, and you will then be shocked at how many you really have. If you are a good unlearner, you can often move very quickly and easily through this stage and immediately enter the transition stage. If you are not a good unlearner, this can be a very rough stage.

New employees find they must deal with four key issues in the initiation stage. First, they come face to face with the gap between what they expected and what they find in the new organization. This leads to stress and frustration that they must cope with. In time, they realize they have to discover the new ways of their new employer and let go of their old ways of working.

Table 1: Key Tasks and Issues of Employment Stages

STAGE	KEY ISSUES
Initiation	REALITY SHOCK Expectation Gap Coping Discovery Letting Go
Transition	SENSE MAKING Norms Breaking In Fitting In Negotiation
Adaptation	CHANGE Acceptance Internalizing Accommodation Commitment

In the transition stage, you can start figuring out the new culture. The best new employees begin this process by letting go of old assumptions on day one. Nothing shocks them because they enter a new organization with a clean slate. More typically, this stage will involve your trying to understand new norms and finding ways to "break in" to groups within the organization. Another part of this stage is finding ways to fit in with new groups so you can make a contribution. Sometimes this also involves negotiating with the organization to make the job fit you better.

The adaptation stage is characterized by change and acceptance of the new culture. This is where you internalize the new protocols and norms so they become part of you instead of having to struggle to remember them. It is here that you become accepted by your colleagues because you have accepted them. Until you reach this stage, you cannot reach your maximum productivity. The key, of course, is *unlearning!* Inevitably, this also requires you to make some accommodations to the organization by adapting to its culture.

First-Year Goals

Although achieving high levels of productivity is certainly an important goal, it is not enough for employment success. Organizations are comprised of groups of people—people who will scrutinize and judge you. Just because you have been hired does not mean that you have been accepted by the people within the organization as "one of them." Your expertise and contributions will not automatically be respected by your colleagues. Although your credentials and previous success may have allowed you to be hired, they are not sufficient to earn acceptance for you. You have to prove yourself all over again. Therefore, earning *acceptance, respect,* and *credibility* should be as important as productivity in your first-year goals. Furthermore, until you earn acceptance, respect, and credibility, it is unlikely that you will be able to perform the tasks of your job at an outstanding level.

Twelve Strategic Steps to Helping "New" Employees Succeed

The twelve-step model presented in figure 1 focuses both on *what* you need to learn in order to succeed in your new position and *how* you need to learn it. This model is based on extensive research and has been field tested in organizations such as J. P. Morgan, Enterprise Rent-A-Car, the U.S. Department of Energy, the U.S. General Services Administration, and the Multiple Sclerosis Society.

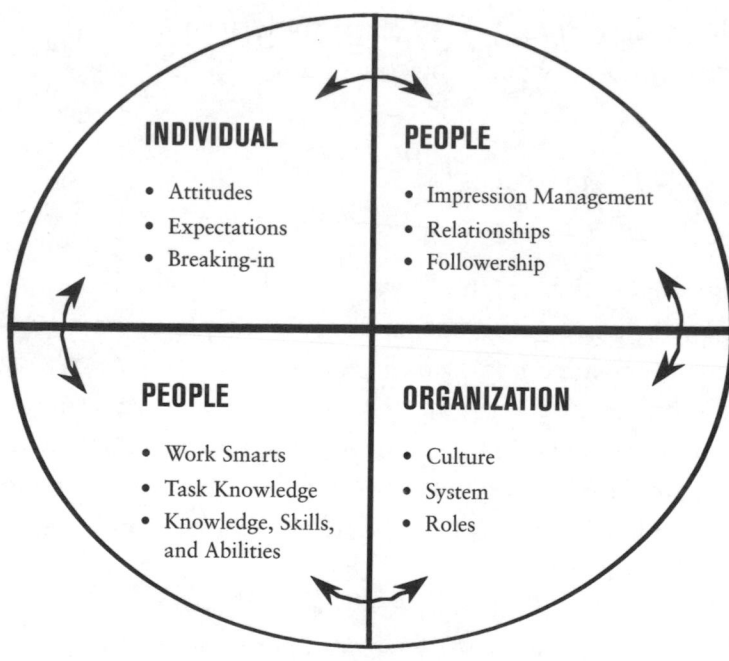

Figure 1: New Employee Learning Tasks

The twelve steps are grouped into four categories, as listed below:

Individual Focus

Step 1: Adopt the right attitudes.

Step 2: Adjust your expectations.

Step 3: Master breaking-in skills.

People Focus

Step 4: Manage the impressions you make.

Step 5: Build effective relationships.

Step 6: Build a strong working relationship with your manager/supervisor.

Organization Focus

Step 7: Understand your organization's culture.

Step 8: Adapt to the organizational system.

Step 9: Understand your new-hire role.

Work Task Focus

Step 10: Develop work smarts.

Step 11: Master the tasks of your job.

Step 12: Acquire the knowledge, skills, and abilities you need.

The first nine steps of this program will help you accomplish the three goals of earning acceptance, earning respect, and earning credibility and set the essential foundation for your success. The last three steps are task-related; they complete the process and enable you to be productive.

Surprised that the task-related steps are last? Make no mistake, you must be proficient at the tasks you are asked to perform. But becoming an outstanding employee requires much more than technical skill or know-how. No matter how brilliant you are or how successful you have been, it is nearly impossible for you to receive an outstanding performance rating at the end of your first year without first mastering the nontask aspects of your new job. And you can't really understand the tasks until you understand the people and the organization.

Three

Step 1: Adopt the Right Attitudes

Your challenge in this step is to identify "success-related attitudes" in your new organization. Identify colleagues who seem successful and respected by others. What are their attitudes toward other people, their jobs, the organization, and the future of the organization? Focus on modeling your attitudes after theirs. Don't make the assumption that the success-related attitudes in your old organization will work the same with your new employer. There will most likely be some overlap, but there will be differences too. A little time spent identifying success-related attitudes can save you from making costly mistakes later. Once you have identified them, work extra hard to cultivate those attitudes and display them while you are new.

Here are some key attitudes that managers in almost every organization like to see in their new employees:

Appropriate humility

Your previous success can leave you feeling overconfident. You must realize that each organization is different and that a successful job change generally requires a healthy dose of humility. Be confident about your potential but humble about how much you need to learn before you can put your experience to work. Your coworkers will respect you more if you have a proper degree of humility.

Readiness for continual learning

It's important to demonstrate that you understand how much you have yet to learn and your willingness to learn it. Take every opportunity you can to learn. If work is a little slow around the office, then study something. Ask questions—before you tell someone what you think the answer is. Don't insist that you're right when your previous learning is challenged. Be open to new learning before you put your experience to work.

Adaptability

Organizational life is full of changes, and new employees need to be flexible. It is almost impossible to know exactly what your new job and organization will be like. In today's world, the most effective employees are those who are flexible, adapt easily, and embrace change.

Respect for the organization

While your new organization may be quite different from your previous one, it is important to demonstrate that you respect it the way it is. Employers generally prefer that new employees respect how business is being done, even if those ways could be improved. Furthermore, if you respect the organization, the people in it are more likely to respect you.

Open-mindedness

Don't bring to your new job preconceived notions about what the organization ought to be like, how business ought to be done, and what you are supposed to do. As a new employee with experience, you are particularly likely to make this mistake. Start with an open mind about the organization and its way of doing business. Be amenable to new ways of thinking and working and open to new experiences.

Commitment

Great organizations are built on highly committed people. A big question on every employer's mind is whether new employees will demonstrate the level of commitment desired. Look for opportunities to show your commitment, even in small ways. Until people are sure of your commitment to your new organization, expect to encounter resistance if you suggest doing things the way they were done in your previous organization.

Strong work ethic

The first year on your new job is a lot harder than later years, so extra effort is required. Go the "extra mile" during the first year to make sure your new employer sees you are a hard worker. Employers know that if someone is willing to work hard, that person will likely succeed.

Positive attitude

Your employer wants employees with a positive approach to work. When you smile and are upbeat, people will want to associate with you. Expect to hear your new colleagues tell you about all the problems and warts of your new organization, but don't get pulled down by this. Keep enough of a positive attitude that you look like a "breath of fresh thinking" to your employer but not so much that you alienate your new colleagues.

Points for Reflection

Look at successful people in your new organization. Identify the attitudes they seem to have in common. These are the success-related attitudes in your organization. Now think about your own attitudes. Which ones helped you to succeed in your previous organization? Which success-related attitudes do you need to develop for your new company? Are they different?

Four

Step 2: Adjust Your Expectations

Frustration is nothing more than the difference between expectations and reality. "But I don't have any expectations," you may say. You might not *think* you have any, but in reality, you do. Everyone goes into a new job with expectations, hopes, and dreams. You probably took your new job because you think that it will fulfill your needs and help you achieve your goals. The problem is that it's very difficult to have a completely correct picture of an organization before you work there. As a result, you will likely find that some of your expectations are not met while others may be exceeded.

In addition, your previous jobs have created a whole host of expectations. You'll discover that many little details you have taken for granted are not the same in your new organization. You may be frustrated that work isn't done the way you've become accustomed to. This is a particularly big problem for people who have been employed for many years in one organization.

As we stated earlier, it is important that you unlearn old habits and expectations. Try to start with as clean a slate as you can. If you are constantly comparing what you are experiencing to a mental checklist of expectations, your new employer is almost certain to come up short in some area. If you can keep your checklist short or change expectations to wishes, then your frustration will be minimized. Granted, this is hard to do, but it is an important step. Many times people find that their new organization is quite good, even if it is not what they thought it would be.

If you find yourself thinking any of the following, you may be experiencing expectation-related frustration and should re-examine your expectations:

- "The way it was done in my old job was better."

- "Things aren't like the interviewer said they would be."

- "Nobody will tell me how things work around here."

- "I wonder if I should have made this change."

- "I thought I was hired for my new ideas."

- "Why didn't anyone tell me about . . . ."

- "I wish I had known all these things before I took the job."

- "Someone should have told me about . . . ."

While each of these could also be a symptom of real problems, in your first year on a new job, they may also be the result of an expectation gap, which will keep you from being truly effective.

Points for Reflection

First, describe your ideal first year on the job. Then, describe what would make you disappointed in your new job. Look at the descriptions carefully. Are they realistic scenarios? Are they likely to happen? What will you do if not everything about your job is as you would like it to be?

Five

Step 3: Master Breaking-in Skills

A s we have stated, entering a new organization or a new job requires special skills, called "breaking-in" skills. Let's look at some key guidelines for being a successful newcomer.

You are an outsider until you prove otherwise

Newcomers often fail to distinguish between being hired and being accepted by the people in the organization. Being accepted takes some time and must be earned. Until you earn acceptance, you will be considered an outsider.

You can't change the system until you are part of it

When an insider criticizes an organization or tries to make changes, it is considered constructive. When an outsider (that's you) criticizes or suggests changes, this probably will be seen as an attack. The presumption is that until you have been a part of the organization for a while, you can't possibly understand it well enough to make constructive criticisms. Experienced employees are particularly likely to want to implement some of their ideas to quickly make a contribution. Remember that many people don't want newcomers to make changes until they learn and respect the way the organization is before they begin suggesting the way the organization *should be*.

Avoid "big splash" strategies

Your experience will enable you to make significant contributions or present new ideas for change. However, if you do that before you have earned acceptance and before you understand your new organization well, you will most likely only embarrass yourself. The quickest way to make a big splash is not to try too soon.

Admitting what you don't know is more important than showing what you do know

What makes the most positive impression, regardless of how much experience you have, is having the wisdom to know how much you need to learn about your new job and new organization. That means keeping your eyes and ears open at first to find out as much as you can about the company and the people in it. It is very easy to ignore the nuances and subtleties of working in your new organization. Demonstrating that you are a good learner will be greatly respected.

Conformity may be more important than individuality

You may well be accustomed to shaping your job and work to fit your personal style, particularly if you have considerable experience. However, as a newcomer you may find that you need to be more of a conformist for a while. First, this shows that you are embracing your new organization's culture. Second, it may take some time to figure out what the acceptable ways are to shape your job to fit you. You will have more opportunities to express your individuality at work in the future.

Build a track record

The old saying is true: Nothing sells like success. Look for projects and tasks that give you opportunities to be successful. Be sure to make the right mistakes—that is, those that come naturally from learning, not those that come from impatience. Early successes will show your employer that he or she made a good decision in hiring you and open the door to more opportunities for success. By doing so, you'll stay on the "success spiral."

Points for Reflection

Describe what you experienced when you were new in your previous job. What good experiences do you remember about being a new employee? What difficult experiences do you remember? What did you do that helped you become a productive employee? What did you do that might have hurt you in becoming a productive employee? What lessons did you learn?

Six

Step 4: Manage the Impressions You Make

No matter what your job, you must place a premium on managing the impressions you make in your first year. As one manager we interviewed said, "You're really in a fishbowl right now. Whenever you start any job, I don't care what it is, there are a lot of people watching you and trying to assess your ability to succeed." Those people include your peers, subordinates, and bosses. Human nature is such that people who make the best early impressions will be the first to be given opportunities to succeed on projects that really matter to the organization and will have the highest visibility.

Everything you do early on will be magnified in its impact. As you progress in the organization, your track record will provide a safety net to help protect you against inevitable mistakes and political gaffes. But in the early months, the impressions and perceptions others have of you count more heavily. Sometimes, even the smallest mistakes are magnified when you're new. Paul, in the opening scenario, may have had good intentions, but because nobody knew him well, his suggestions were taken out of context.

The most common mistake new employees with experience make is to assume that their previous track record will automatically be taken into account by the new organization. This is an easy mistake to make because your track record is what enabled you to be hired, and it meant a lot during the interview process. Once you're on the job, however, your colleagues and teammates may take a different view. They want to see what you can do *for them*, not what you did for somebody else. Thus, in some sense your track record will be discounted by your colleagues until you show that you can have the same successes in your new organization. Consider this part of the new employee "test." After you pass the test, your track record will be more meaningful to others.

It is hard to define precisely what the "right" impression is since every organization is different. That's why the first challenge in making a good impression is having the professional savvy to figure out what the organization wants to see. Since your colleagues won't know you well yet, your second challenge is to pay attention to the actions that create strong, positive first impressions. Little things that you don't think are very important can create impressions and perceptions. Often they provide the only information other people can use to make early judgments about you. For example, volunteering to help on a project, making an extra effort to learn new skills quickly, or taking time to learn about your coworkers' jobs will mean more than you might think. Make the right impressions and people will want to be associated with you, get to know you better, and help you. That's getting on the success spiral.

Remember, it's a lot easier to get noticed for what you do wrong than what you do right. You should evaluate everything you do as to how it will look to people who know nothing about you but are going to put a label on you. Find opportunities to do what you know people will like to see and avoid doing anything that could be misinterpreted.

Points for Reflection

Identify at least three ways you have made positive impressions as a new employee in previous jobs. Then, identify at least three instances in which you were surprised that you made negative impressions in previous jobs. Next, identify at least five strategies you can use to make positive impressions quickly in your new job. Finally, identify what you need to be careful about so as not to create negative impressions.

Seven

Step 5: Build Effective Relationships

Organizations aren't just collections of tasks and duties; they are people working together toward a common goal. People shape an organization, determine how work gets done, decide your future, and determine the success of an organization. Every job, no matter how technical, will require you to be successful at working with, through, and around people. In addition, the only way you will learn how to become successful in an organization is from people.

Picture a typical new employee: sitting in his or her office, working long hours to meet a project deadline, taking manuals and books home at night to learn more, skipping lunch to make sure the work is done just right. If this sounds like a smart new employee to you, you're only partially right. Much of what you need to know about office procedures, the organization's culture, and how to sell your ideas is not written down and can be learned only from other people in the organization.

It then follows that building good relationships is the only way that you can be successful in your job. If you don't build strong relationships where people like you and want to teach you and help you, it is almost guaranteed that you will not become an outstanding performer. That's why you have to put a premium on relationship building in the early months of a new job.

Here are some tips for building effective relationships at work:

Make building strong working relationships a priority

Take the time to develop relationships with as many people as possible at all levels of the organization. Make this a priority on your to-do list. Meet people, go to lunch with them, have coffee with them, and *listen!* If you are an introverted type, force yourself to mingle with your colleagues.

Demonstrate good interpersonal communication and relationship-building skills

Focus on communicating and working well with people. Remind yourself of the fundamentals of interpersonal communication, how to avoid or manage conflict, and how to see others' perspectives. Make a special effort in the early months to respect and work with all types of people. While this may sound basic, it's an easy task to overlook if you were at your previous job long enough to become comfortable in a network of relationships. Remember, you are starting over.

Focus on teamwork

It is especially important to show your new colleagues that you can be a good team player. Being a team player means learning to share your success, involve others, become less competitive and possessive about your ideas, and be open to others' ideas.

Network, network, network

One of the hardest parts about joining a new organization is that you have to build a new network of contacts, resources, advisers, and sources of information. If you are changing jobs within the same organization, you may be able to tap your old network. However, if you are changing organizations and have considerable experience, this task may be particularly challenging because it may have been a while since you had to develop new contacts.

Find a mentor, coach, or sponsor

Every new employee, no matter what level, needs the guidance of more senior colleagues. If a structured mentoring program is available in your organization, take advantage of it. If not, seek out more experienced employees who seem to have an interest in helping you. Let them guide you in understanding how your experience fits or does not fit your new organization. Be careful to choose people who seem to be respected in the organization.

Points for Reflection

List at least five groups of people who you think will be particularly important to your success in your new job. For each, list specific steps you will take to build good working relationships with them. Be sure to consider peers, support staff, other members of your work group, resource networks, senior management, and other groups.

Eight

Step 6: Build a Strong Working Relationship with Your Manager/Supervisor

It may have been a while since you've had to adjust to a new boss, particularly if you were at another company for a long time. One possible scenario might be that you worked for the same person for years and became very accustomed to his or her ways. Without even thinking about it, your natural inclination will be to project that person's likes and dislikes on your new boss. Another scenario might be that you moved around to various jobs and bosses within your previous organization.

Most likely, you consider yourself somewhat experienced at adjusting to new managers. What you might have forgotten is how much you already knew about a new boss at your previous organization and how much he or she knew about you before you began working for that person. You probably heard a lot about the person through the office "grapevine" and could easily ask around to find out his or her preferences. The reality now is that you are starting fresh with a boss that you know nothing at all about and who knows nothing about you. The adjustment can be bigger than you think.

To help you remember everything you have to find out about your boss, here are some key questions you need to answer to get your relationship off to a strong start:

- How much information does your boss like to have?

- Does your boss like to receive regular updates or just know about problems?

- Does your boss like to be offered solutions to problems or be part of the problem-solving process?

- What are your boss's standards in terms of work quality?

- What is your boss's agenda—wants, needs, and expectations?

- How can you best support your boss?

- Which of the tasks you are assigned are most likely to get your boss in trouble if done poorly?

- What are the demands on your boss's time?

- What are the critical resources you can help your boss obtain or conserve?

- How can you help your boss be more efficient and productive?

- When do you need to be most available?

- How can you make yourself indispensable?

Second, you need to revisit some basics about how you relate to your boss to make sure your previous ways are appropriate for your new boss:

- Which decisions does your boss like to make, and which ones will he or she delegate?

- In what way is your boss most comfortable giving you feedback?

- In which areas is it particularly important that you stay flexible?

- How much ownership of your job does your boss like to see?

- What level of independence does your boss expect of you?

- If you disagree with your boss, how should you handle this?

- What is the best way to get help from your boss if you need it?

- When your boss makes requests or gives instructions, what should you do to exceed his or her expectations?

- How should you respond when you are given an assignment?

Because of your experience, you know how important it is to have a strong relationship with your boss. However, you have also built up a list of assumptions about how that should be done based on other organizations. In the early months on your new job, you need to recheck all those assumptions. Also, don't be surprised if adapting requires you to call on some skills you have not used for some time.

Points for Reflection

Make a list of what you think you should do to have a strong working relationship with your boss. These are your assumptions. Where did you learn them? Are they applicable in your new organization? How can you check them to be sure? If you showed your list to your new boss, would he or she agree with it?

Nine

Step 7: Understand Your Organization's Culture

Every company has its own unique personality or "culture," also known as "around-hereisms." You'll hear them every day: "We don't do things like that around here," "We like to see people working hard around here," "The boss likes people around here to show up early in the morning," and so on. These rules and norms, many of which are unspoken and informal, will shape everything you do in an organization from how you work with people to what you wear to work. Culture defines *how* you do *what* you were hired to do.

You should remember two basic rules about culture. First, employers want employees who "fit" an organization's culture and enthusiastically embrace it. That doesn't mean that everyone should be a clone, but all organizations have limits on individuality. Second, initially your challenge is to show that you can unlearn the norms from your old organization's culture and fit into the new organization's culture. If you don't take time to understand the new culture, you are almost assured of making many dumb and embarrassing mistakes that will hurt your career.

Culture leaves an indelible imprint on employees. Thus, the culture from your previous job or organization likely shaped you more than you may be consciously aware of. You will need to work at unlearning the old culture so you can learn to operate effectively within your new culture.

Here are some critical elements of culture to pay attention to:

- Mission of the organization

- Guiding philosophies

- Basic values and norms

- Behavioral expectations

- Work ethic

- What gets rewarded

- Social norms

- Success factors

- Management norms

- Management philosophies

- Ethical standards

- Sacred beliefs and events

- Dress code

- Attitudes of employees

- Communication norms

- Work norms

- Office climate

How can these affect you? Consider one new employee who was quick to criticize a project only to find out that it was originally proposed by one of his senior mangers, who still believed in it. Paul, in the opening scenario, alienated people because he didn't understand how important being a team player was. Another new employee didn't attend safety meetings and continued to violate safety rules, not realizing that workplace safety was highly valued by the company. Another didn't understand that one office protocol was never to discuss an issue with your boss's boss without first informing your boss. Imagine her surprise when she was reprimanded for "going over her boss's head."

How do you learn culture? It's hard because it is rarely written down and most people can't explain it to you directly. For the most part, you can learn it by observation. Pay attention to "the way things are done around here." Watch your colleagues and pay attention to what they spend their time on. Learn what the norms and values of the organization are by noting how others behave. Find out what the basic mission and philosophy of the organization is by asking. Understand what people expect of you, particularly regarding the accepted work ethic and social norms. Pay attention to the political climate and how people communicate and work together. Remember that building good relationships is the key to understanding the culture.

All of this and more are part of the organization's culture. To be successful, you must take time to learn it before getting too adventurous. Don't let the culture you come from hinder your learning of the new culture. Embrace and respect your new organization's culture. Find ways to fit in, and realize that you can't change your organization until you are part if it.

Other than talking to people, you can learn the culture by observing or researching the following:

- People's activities

- Organizational priorities

- Legends and heroes

- Rites and rituals

- Physical setting

- The organization's structure

- Policies and procedures

- The organization's history

- What is rewarded

- Career paths and progression

- Leaders' behavior

Points for Reflection

Create a worksheet with two columns. In the left column, list words that describe the culture at your previous employer's. In the right column, list words that describe the culture at your new employer's. What are the similarities? What are the differences? To which of the differences will you have the most difficulty adjusting?

Ten

Step 8: Adapt to the Organizational System

A s an experienced employee, you have an advantage in that you are accustomed to the way organizations operate and how to be effective in them. However, you need to revisit two key areas to make sure you start out right: organizational politics and the informal way business is done.

Organizational politics

As you know, everything that happens within an organization includes politics. Politics is just the way things get done when people work together. It can be nasty and vicious but usually is not. It's the process of sharing resources, sharing power, and influencing others. Take time to define your new organization's power and political structure, identify the "players" within the organization, and select the battles that are worth fighting. You need to know what the controversial political positions are and the consequences of treading on this dangerous ground.

Here are some key questions to answer about your organization's politics:

- What are the important compromises to make?

- Who needs to be involved in making decisions?

- Who are the key "players" relevant to your work?

- How do people negotiate?

- Which battles are worth fighting and which ones are futile?

- Where are the coalitions of people who agree with you on an issue?

- On which issues is it dangerous to "go out on a limb" by yourself?

- What are the controversial political issues?

- Who has the power and who wants it?

Think of politics in terms of playing with poker chips: you get some and you spend some. Unfortunately, when you change jobs you often give up much of the political clout you may have had in your old position. Thus, proceed cautiously in your first year and build up your chips through good performance.

Getting results

Organizations establish formal policies and procedures, but the people in them develop their own informal structures and methods that facilitate work. These are the "backdoor" ways of finding information, the shortcuts around the cumbersome purchasing system, the informal agreements among departments to expedite work flow. Thousands of procedures and ways of doing things also exist that are never documented and simply evolve over time. These informal, unwritten ways of doing business make organizations more productive but are likely to differ from those in your old job. You may be surprised when you realize how many informal ways of doing business you had taken for granted. If you want to get results in your new job, you will have to learn how work "really gets done around here." And the only way to do that is to watch people and ask questions.

Points for Reflection ────────────────────

Suppose you had to teach a class on "learning the ropes" to a group of recent college graduates hired by your employer. What would you tell these new employees? How would you tell them to figure out the politics of the organization? What would you tell them about how to learn how work really gets done? How would you tell them to decipher the unwritten rules of the organization? Now, take your own advice.

Eleven

Step 9: Understand Your New-Hire Role

Nobody really likes being new in an organization. It can be uncomfortable and frustrating, especially if you have not been new in a while. What we are suggesting is a new way of thinking: practicing the art of being new. We have found that it's just as important to learn how to be new as it is to be experienced. The more you understand and accept being new and the better you become in the new employee role, the quicker you can leave it behind. This is contrary to traditional thinking, which says you need to *stop* acting like a new employee as quickly as possible. However, effective new employees understand the importance of the transition period. They accept the newcomer role, understand the special rules for newcomers, and vigorously attack the tasks of learning about the organization and becoming accepted.

Here are a few of the guidelines you should follow as a new employee.

Don't resist new employee "dues"

Every organization has certain tasks that new employees are saddled with. You probably know them as "rites of passage" or "paying your dues." Sometimes you get the worst tasks on a team or project. Sometimes you are assigned all the tasks nobody else really wants to do. Often you get the worst desk and office.

Don't take it personally

Sometimes these are done as a little bit of hazing and sometimes they are done just because someone has to do these tasks. Everyone was once new and was also treated this way. If you resist or complain, you will only create resentment because other people won't understand why you can't put up with this treatment like they did.

If you are treated this way, relax. Remember that this is a transition period, not your entire career. We guarantee you that you will win respect by fitting into your role, whatever it is, and doing your work to the best of your ability as cheerfully as possible.

Understand the bigger picture

Many new employees fail to quickly learn the big picture in their organizations. They develop "tunnel vision," focusing mostly on their own needs, interests, and jobs. Your new job is very important to you and consumes a lot of your energy and time. However, your organization has *many* other priorities that are equally as important as or more important than helping you do your job well. Look at the bigger picture. What might seem vitally important to you may not be as important to everyone else. Be professionally savvy enough to recognize this and take responsibility for yourself.

Find your niche

It can be frustrating to be new without having a well-defined role. Take time to look carefully at what role the people in your organization want you to play. Do they want you to be an assistant for a while before you take on more significant responsibility? Do they need you to cover for someone who is out for major surgery? Do they want you to spend six months going to school? Or do they need you to step in and take charge quickly?

Many new employees create problems for themselves and for others by trying to force the organization to fit their own plans. Forget what *you* think your role should be and figure out what the *organization* wants your role to be. Then, fill that role willingly and to the best of your ability. You will earn great respect for it.

Points for Reflection

Think about your current role as a new employee. How would you describe it? What would you like it to be? Is there a discrepancy? Is that discrepancy affecting you at work? Do you need to do something to either make the role better or adjust to it the way it is?

Twelve

Step 10: Develop Work Smarts

As a new employee with experience, developing work smarts may not be a very difficult step. If your new job is very similar to your previous position, the skills you mastered there may be directly transferable. On the other hand, if you are making a career transition to a different type of job, you'll probably need to make certain adjustments or learn new skills. For example, if you have been in positions where you worked on a few big projects at a time but are taking a position with operational responsibilities, you may find that the time management skills needed are quite different.

Consider this section a quick checklist to see if there are any professional skills that you need to improve. These may include

- managing your time efficiently

- setting priorities

- juggling multiple projects

- writing memos, letters, and reports

- making oral presentations

- managing work flow

- managing and participating in meetings

- selling your ideas

- working with secretaries and administrative assistants

- organizing your work and office

- setting realistic deadlines

- producing the right level of quality

Points for Reflection

As an accomplished professional, you may have little work to do in this area. On the other hand, you may find some of your skills in need of retooling to fit the new organization. Give yourself a grade on each of the above items. Which ones do you need to work on so you fit in better?

Thirteen

Step 11: Master the Tasks of Your Job

While the emphasis in this book has been on the nontask elements of your job, don't be fooled into thinking that task performance is not important. Your employer *definitely* expects you to perform your job tasks with a high level of proficiency.

When you have completed the previous ten steps, you will be in a position to really master the tasks of your job. You will be able to fully understand the tasks, the relationship between your tasks and the entire organization, how work really gets done, and whom to work with to accomplish the organization's goals. Now you simply have to perform your tasks well.

Typically, your employer will provide some training to get you started. Don't take it lightly, even if you aren't convinced that you need the training. If nothing else, it will serve as a refresher course. More than likely, you'll discover new ways to apply what you have previously learned.

Points for Reflection ——————————————————

Think differently for a minute about the tasks of your job. Assume you had mastered the technical parts of the job. What else would you need to do to be more effective? Are you producing the results the organization wants? How can you make your technical knowledge more effective?

Fourteen

Step 12: Acquire the Knowledge, Skills, and Abilities You Need

D espite your experience, you will likely find that you lack certain skills and abilities that you need. Here's how you can acquire the knowledge and skills to do your job better:

Don't be embarrassed to ask for training or help

As an experienced professional, you may feel that you should not need much training. Don't let this feeling stop you from taking advantage of training made available to new employees. The new employee period provides you a license to ask questions and pursue training that you will not have later. Take advantage of it.

Become a continual learner

Take the responsibility and initiative to guide your own development. At this point, you should have a very good idea as to what type of development you need. Sit down with your manager and colleagues and ask for their input. Pay careful attention to your performance reviews. Then devise a plan to guide your development. If you have spare time, which often happens with new employees, use it to learn something new. Nobody will force you to develop. It is your responsibility.

Points for Reflection

Continual learning is a necessity in today's work world. In what areas do you need to develop to do your current job? To prepare for your future positions?

Fifteen

Taking Responsibility for Your Success

I t is *your* responsibility to make the transition to your new job a success, not your employer's. Invest your time and energy in making your first year a successful one. It's an investment that will definitely pay off in the future. Everyone goes through many new-employee-type transitions during a career, so learning how to make this twelve-step process work will benefit you throughout your life.

Putting these steps into practice takes effort and time. Unfortunately, few jobs allow you to work through these steps one at a time. Instead, you'll be involved with all of them at once, at least to some degree. This is especially true for experienced employees because there is more pressure for you to "hit the ground running." Use the steps to set priorities on what you need to learn. Steps 1–3 should be your first priority and can be accomplished (for the most part) before you start work. Making the right impressions and building relationships (steps 4–6) should be your next priority. Learning the culture, adapting to the organizational system, and understanding your role (steps 7–9) will follow naturally from your relationships. Finally, your task performance (steps 10–12) will be the next priority as you move along in your first year, the "honeymoon" ends, and people begin to look for a level of performance commensurate with your experience.

Each organization is a little different, so the priorities of the steps may have to be varied. For example, if you start work when the organization is trying to meet a major deadline, you may have to focus on tasks before you are ready and may not have time to build relationships. However, when the deadline is met, you'll need to backtrack since each of the twelve steps must be successfully accomplished. *Do not skip any step when changing organizations.*

Tracking Your Progress

On the next page is an inventory to help you track your progress. This is a handy tool to review each step and chart your progress through the three stages. Use it about once a month to make sure you are focusing on each step and developing as fast as you can.

Tracking Your Progress

This inventory will help you measure your progress in your new job. Complete the inventory about once a month to remind yourself of these important issues as well as to assess your progress.

Consider each of the twelve steps separately. Think about where you are most of the time with regard to each one and, using the answer key, place an "X" in the circle that most closely matches your evaluation of yourself.

Answer Key:

① I am discovering what the organization is really like.
② I am trying to make sense of what I've seen.
③ I am beginning to understand what the organization wants and why.
④ I am trying to figure out how to make changes.
⑤ I am in the process of changing myself in order to better fit in.
⑥ I have successfully made the changes necessary to fit in.

Adaptation Task	Initiation (Reality Shock)	Transition (Sense Making)	Adaptation (Change)
Attitudes	① ②	③ ④	⑤ ⑥
Expectations	① ②	③ ④	⑤ ⑥
Breaking-in Skills	① ②	③ ④	⑤ ⑥
Impression Management	① ②	③ ④	⑤ ⑥
Relationship Building	① ②	③ ④	⑤ ⑥
Manager/Supervisor	① ②	③ ④	⑤ ⑥
Organizational Culture	① ②	③ ④	⑤ ⑥
Organizational System	① ②	③ ④	⑤ ⑥
Roles	① ②	③ ④	⑤ ⑥
Work Smarts	① ②	③ ④	⑤ ⑥
Tasks	① ②	③ ④	⑤ ⑥
Knowledge, Skills, and Abilities	① ②	③ ④	⑤ ⑥

Issues and Challenges

Many experienced new employees find the transition to a new job challenging. The more years that have passed since you were a new employee, the harder the transition is likely to be. Here are some common issues that arise.

"The people I work with don't understand what it's like to be new"

This is probably true. It takes only a year or two on a job for someone to forget what it's like to be new. Indeed, you may have forgotten yourself. Few managers receive training in how to bring new employees into an organization. Don't expect anyone to automatically know what you need. Communicate your needs in a nondemanding way.

"I don't like the new employee feeling"

Nobody really likes feeling new, so the first year on a new job can be a very insecure and uncomfortable time. Remember that the quickest way to end the uncomfortable feeling is to learn to do a great job at being new.

"I thought I was hired to contribute my new ideas, not to fit in"

Remember that the advice in this book is just to get you started. You won't always have to fit in as much as you do now. However, fitting in now will earn you the right to create your own individual style later.

"I'm not as happy as I thought I would be"

It is very common for new employees to feel a little disappointed during the first year, usually because their expectations are not met. Often, there is a burst of happiness and enthusiasm in the beginning, followed by a letdown, and then—here's the good news—a return of enjoyment and satisfaction once the adjustment phase is past.

"I can't handle it all"

Sometimes you are thrown into a pile of problems or get too much to do too fast and it all seems very confusing. Try to relax. Even the most experienced employees sometimes feel overwhelmed in a new job. It takes time to settle in, but the situation will improve. Don't be afraid to ask for help and don't expect more of yourself than everyone else does.

"I didn't think experienced new hires had to worry about these steps"

Remember, even CEOs have to think and work differently when they are new, and even CEOs fail because they don't fit a new culture. At no point in your career can you stop worrying about the art of being new.

Conclusion

Making a Successful Transition

Once you accept the unique nature of the transition to a new job, this period can be lots of fun, very exciting, and a terrific stage in a successful career. The twelve steps discussed in this book will remind you of new employee tasks you may have forgotten, help you make sense of a critical career stage, build a solid foundation for advancement, and get a fast start. Most importantly, they will keep you from spoiling lots of hard work by making mistakes and missing the rewards you have earned.

The advice given here represents a conservative, safe approach to starting a new position. Most new employees have told us that as they got to know their new organizations, they found areas where they didn't have to be so conservative. Each of them reported something a little different about his or her organization, but nobody has ever said he or she made mistakes with this approach. The twelve-step approach will keep you from making mistakes in the beginning and put you on the road to building respect, acceptance, and credibility. Few employers will fault you for a conservative start.

If approached correctly, this can be a wonderful time in your professional life. Have fun, work hard, enjoy your success, and be the best new employee you know how to be. *Good luck!*

Index

Index

Related Books

How to Succeed in Your First Job: Tips for New College Graduates, Elwood F. Holton III and Sharon S. Naquin

This book teaches new college graduates *what* they need to learn and *how* to learn it. It uses the twelve-part new employee development model to teach recent graduates how to make the transition from college to work. The emphasis is on helping readers learn how college not only fails to fully prepare them for the workplace but also countertrains them so the transition is even more difficult. Readers learn key tasks within the twelve-part model that will help make their transition smoother.

Learning about a new organization is a process that is fundamentally different from learning in a classroom. Even if employees know what to learn, they also need help learning how to learn about the organizations they've just joined. This book first presents an interview protocol that newcomers can use to interview their colleagues and supervisors about topics critical to new employees. Worksheets are also provided to help them analyze the information they collect using the twelve-part new employee development model. At the conclusion, readers develop a personal action and development plan. Analysis sheets offer the perfect tool for new employees and managers to discuss success factors and begin a customized development process for each individual.

Helping Your New Employee Succeed: Tips for Managers of New College Graduates, Elwood F. Holton III and Sharon S. Naquin

This book is the perfect guide for supervisors of new employees. The twelve-part new employee development model is used to teach supervisors and managers what they need to teach new employees. In most organizations, the manager or supervisor of a new employee is perhaps the most important person in creating a successful transition from college to the workplace. The manager either has direct control over many of the twelve transition tasks or can create successful learning opportunities for the ones they don't control. Yet few managers have been taught how to help a new employee enter an organization even though the potential costs of not doing it right are considerable. Furthermore, most managers have worked long enough to have forgotten what a new employee experiences. In today's labor markets, retention of key talent is essential. This book helps supervisors know what new employees experience and what they need to be taught to successfully acclimate to the organization.

About the Authors

Elwood F. Holton III, Ed.D., is a professor of human resource development (HRD) at Louisiana State University, where he also coordinates the HRD programs and serves as executive director of the Center for Leadership Development. He is also the im-mediate past president of the Academy of Human Resource Development. He consults with public, private, and nonprofit organizations on all types of human resource development, leadership development, and performance improvement projects. Holton has developed and refined his twelve-step model through numerous presentations to new employee and human resource practitioner groups, including consulting engagements in organizations such as J. P. Morgan, Enterprise Rent-A-Car, the U.S. Department of Energy, the U.S. General Services Administration, and the Multiple Sclerosis Society. He is the author of 11 books and more than 150 articles.

Sharon S. Naquin, Ph.D., is the director of the Office of Human Resource Development Research and an assistant professor of human resource development at Louisiana State University. She has eleven years of experience in corporate human resources. In those roles, she has recruited, hired, and trained hundreds of new employees. As a consultant, she has worked on all types of human resource, employee training, and performance improvement problems. She has also published in the areas of dispositional effects on adult learning in the workplace, organizational needs analysis, leadership development, performance improvement systems, community workforce development systems, and management development evaluation.

Berrett-Koehler Publishers

BERRETT-KOEHLER is an independent publisher of books, periodicals, and other publications at the leading edge of new thinking and innovative practice on work, business, management, leadership, stewardship, career development, human resources, entrepreneurship, and global sustainability.

Since the company's founding in 1992, we have been committed to supporting the movement toward a more enlightened world of work by publishing books, periodicals, and other publications that help us to integrate our values with our work and work lives, and to create more humane and effective organizations.

We have chosen to focus on the areas of work, business, and organizations, because these are central elements in many people's lives today. Furthermore, the work world is going through tumultuous changes, from the decline of job security to the rise of new structures for organizing people and work. We believe that change is needed at all levels—individual, organizational, community, and global—and our publications address each of these levels.

We seek to create new lenses for understanding organizations, to legitimize topics that people care deeply about but that current business orthodoxy censors or considers secondary to bottom-line concerns, and to uncover new meaning, means, and ends for our work and work lives.

See next page for other books from Berrett-Koehler Publishers

More books from Berrett-Koehler

301 Ways
to Have Fun at Work

Dave Hemsath and Leslie Yerkes, Illustrated by
Dan McQuillen

In this entertaining and comprehensive guide,
Hemsath and Yerkes show readers how to have fun
at work—everyday. Written for anyone who works in
any type of organization, *301 Ways to Have Fun at
Work* provides more than 300 ideas for creating a dynamic, fun-filled
work environment.

Paperback, 300 pages • ISBN 1-57675-019-1 CIP
Item #50191-349 $14.95

The Power of Purpose
Creating Meaning in Your Life and Work

Richard J. Leider

Concise and easy to read, and including numerous
stories of people living on purpose, *The Power of
Purpose* is an original guide to discovering the
work you love to do.

Hardcover, 170 pages • ISBN 1-57675-021-3 CIP
Item #50213-349 $20.00

Audiotape, 2 cassettes • ISBN 1-57453-215-4
Item #32154-349 $17.95

Repacking Your Bags
Lighten Your Load for the Rest of Your Life

Richard J. Leider and David A. Shapiro

Learn how to find the fulfillment that's missing in
your life. This practical guide will teach you to
balance the demands of work, love, and place to
create and live your own vision of success.

Paperback, 234 pages• ISBN 1-881052-87-7 CIP
Item #52877-349 $15.95

Hardcover • ISBN 1-881052-67-2 CIP Item #52672-349 $21.95

Audiotape, 2 cassettes • ISBN 1-57453-027-5

Berrett-Koehler Publishers
PO Box 565, Williston, VT 05495-9900
Call toll-free! **800-929-2929** 7 am-12 midnight

Or fax your order to 802-864-7627
For fastest service order online: **www.bkconnection.com**